XTREME ADVENTURE

CAVING

BY S.L. HAMILTON

Visit us at
www.abdopublishing.com

Published by ABDO Publishing Company, PO Box 398166, Minneapolis, MN 55439.
Copyright ©2014 by Abdo Consulting Group, Inc. International copyrights reserved in all countries. No part of this book may be reproduced in any form without written permission from the publisher. A&D Xtreme™ is a trademark and logo of ABDO Publishing Company.

Printed in the United States of America, North Mankato, Minnesota.
092013
012014

Editor: John Hamilton
Graphic Design: Sue Hamilton
Cover Design: Sue Hamilton
Cover Photo: Getty Images
Interior Photos: AlaskaStock-pgs 22 & 23; AP-pgs 10-11; Corbis-pgs 6-7, 16-17, 24 (inset) & 27; Getty Images-pgs 8-9, 12-13, 14-15, 15 (inset), 20-21, 24-25, 29 (top & center); Glow Images-pgs 4-5, 18-19, 21 & 29 (top inset); Lawrence Goldman-pg 21 (inset); National Geographic-pg 32; National Park Service-pg 29 (bottom left and right); Ron Niebrugge-pg 26; Thinkstock-pgs 1, 2-3, 28 (bottom left & second from left) & 30-31; U.S. Geological Survey-pg 28 (bottom right); W.Tucker-pg 28 (bottom second from right).

ABDO Booklinks
Web sites about Xtreme Adventure are featured on our Book Links pages. These links are routinely monitored and updated to provide the most current information available.
Web site: www.abdopublishing.com

Library of Congress Control Number: 2013946157

Cataloging-in-Publication Data

Hamilton, S.L.
 Caving / S.L. Hamilton.
  p. cm. -- (Xtreme adventure)
Includes index.
ISBN 978-1-62403-210-3
1. Caving--Juvenile literature.   I. Title.
796.52--dc23

2013946157

CONTENTS

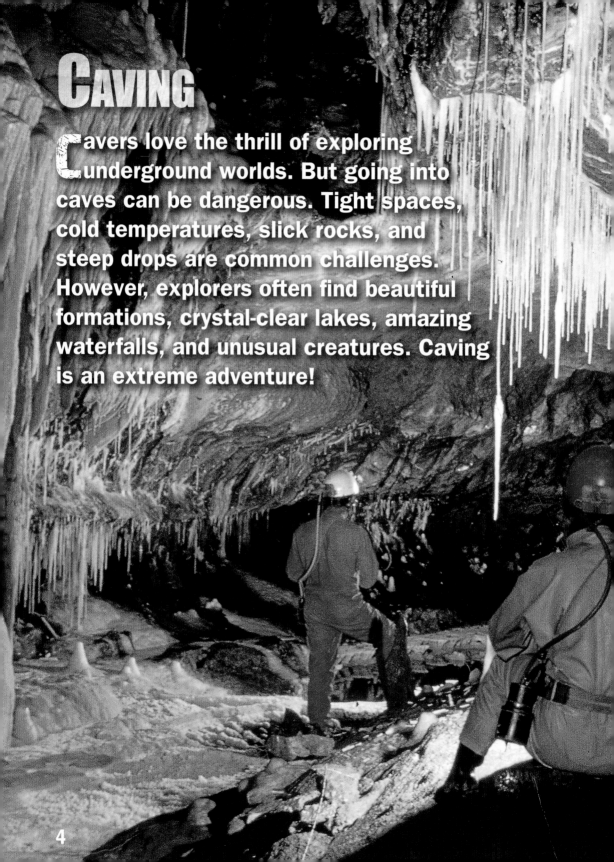

CAVING

Cavers love the thrill of exploring underground worlds. But going into caves can be dangerous. Tight spaces, cold temperatures, slick rocks, and steep drops are common challenges. However, explorers often find beautiful formations, crystal-clear lakes, amazing waterfalls, and unusual creatures. Caving is an extreme adventure!

XTREME FACT– Caving is also called spelunking or potholing.

CLOTHING & EQUIPMENT

Cavers wear a base layer of warm clothes covered by a two-piece wetsuit or a waterproof oversuit. On their feet they wear wool socks and strong leather or rubber boots. Sturdy leather gloves and knee pads are smart "extras." A harness or load-bearing belt is used to carry extra supplies.

XTREME FACT – Cavers carry either electric (battery-powered) or gas (acetylene) lamps. An electric lamp may run up to 12 hours. A carbide lamp, which runs on acetylene gas, is lighter weight, but runs a shorter period of time.

A helmet is very important. It protects an explorer's head. It is equipped with a light that allows a caver to keep both hands free.

Ropes and ladders are the main equipment needed for caving. While most equipment is simple, knowing how to place it and how to move safely into and through a cave takes skill and knowledge.

XTREME FACT– Well-equipped cavers carry first-aid kits, survival bags, whistles for communication, and at least one backup light source.

Cavers must not only protect themselves, but they must also protect the caves they enter. Caves are fragile places. Formations that took thousands of years to create may be destroyed in seconds.

DANGERS

Caving is a dangerous, and sometimes deadly, adventure. An explorer may suffer broken bones from a slip or fall. Caves sometimes collapse. Falling rocks are always a danger. Rain outside the cave may cause flash flooding inside.

Cavers can die from being crushed, drowning, freezing, falling, and from getting lost or stuck inside a cave. Yet cavers are drawn to this extreme adventure. They see areas never before explored by another human being. It's an adventure they can't resist.

XTREME FACT – The most important caving rules are never go into a cave alone and always tell someone your planned route and when you expect to return.

LIMESTONE CAVES

Limestone caves are usually formed by rocks being worn away by groundwater. It is estimated that 90 percent of caves in the world are limestone caves. Kentucky's Mammoth Cave is by far the longest limestone cave in the world.

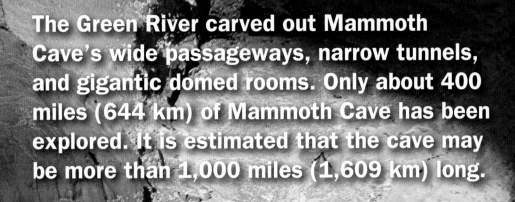

The Green River carved out Mammoth Cave's wide passageways, narrow tunnels, and gigantic domed rooms. Only about 400 miles (644 km) of Mammoth Cave has been explored. It is estimated that the cave may be more than 1,000 miles (1,609 km) long.

Mammoth Cave is part of the United States National Park system. Several miles of the cave are explored each year. Visitors may take various tours of explored areas.

New Mexico's Lechuguilla Cave is the deepest known limestone cave in the United States. It is 1,604 feet (489 m) deep. Lechuguilla (lech-uh-gee-uh) is part of Carlsbad Caverns National Park. Lechuguilla Cave is known for its amazing gypsum stalactite formations.

Experienced cavers continue to explore and map Lechuguilla Cave's many passageways.

XTREME FACT – Lechuguilla Cave was formed by sulfuric acid bubbling up from the ground and mixing with water to dissolve the limestone from the bottom up.

SANDSTONE CAVES

Sandstone caves are created by wind and rain erosion. They are usually not very deep. They are found in regions with large sandstone deposits, such as Minnesota and Wisconsin.

XTREME FACT – Ancient people, such as some of the Anasazi, lived in sandstone caves in Nevada's Valley of Fire and Colorado's Mesa Verde.

Sandstone caves sometimes form in deserts and cliffs, such as those found in the American Southwest and Australia. Some are quite beautiful. For cavers, it is often the journey to reach these caves that makes the adventure so extreme.

LAVA TUBE CAVES

Lava tube caves form when a volcano's lava flow cools from the outside. If the inside remains molten, the material may flow out, leaving behind a hollow tube. These caves have formations made from the dripping and splashing of lava.

Well-known lava tube caves are found in Iceland, Oregon, and Hawaii. Kazumura Cave, on Hawaii's Big Island, is more than 37 miles (60 km) long. It was discovered in the mid-1990s and is one of the longest lava tube caves in the world. Cavers love to be the first people to set foot into lava tubes formed ages ago.

SEA CAVES

Sea caves are also known as littoral caves. They are found along coastlines where waves strike weak points in the rocks and erosion occurs. Small in size, sea caves are usually reached by using a boat or kayak. Many explorers go in when the tide goes out. Cavers must keep track of the water levels so they are not trapped inside.

– *The longest littoral cave is Painted Cave, off the coast of California. It is 1,200 feet (366 m) long. It is tiny by limestone cave standards, but huge for a sea cave. Painted Cave got its name because of the rocks, lichens, and algae that make it look so colorful.*

Painted Cave

ICE & GLACIER CAVES

An ice cave is any type of cave that has some ice in it all year long. Cavers exploring the below-freezing cold zone look for icicles, ice columns, ice-stalagmites, needle ice, frozen waterfalls, and ponded water, which is surface water that has frozen into a clear mass.

A glacier cave is a cave made entirely of ice. It is created when meltwater runs through a glacier and wears away enough ice to form a cave and passageways inside. Mendenhall Glacier near Juneau, Alaska, has an ice cave. Shapes and colors vary, but it is often a world of blues and whites.

Boots with crampons, ice axes, and gloves are needed to explore ice caves.

SINKHOLES & CENOTES

Sinkholes are deep holes in the ground. If the sinkhole is filled with water, it is called a cenote (seh-NOH-tay), which is Spanish for "natural well." Sinkholes and cenotes form when the ground collapses. The collapse may be caused by a cave falling in on itself or by man-made changes to the ground, such as mines or broken water pipes.

An aerial view of sinkholes and cenotes in Mexico.

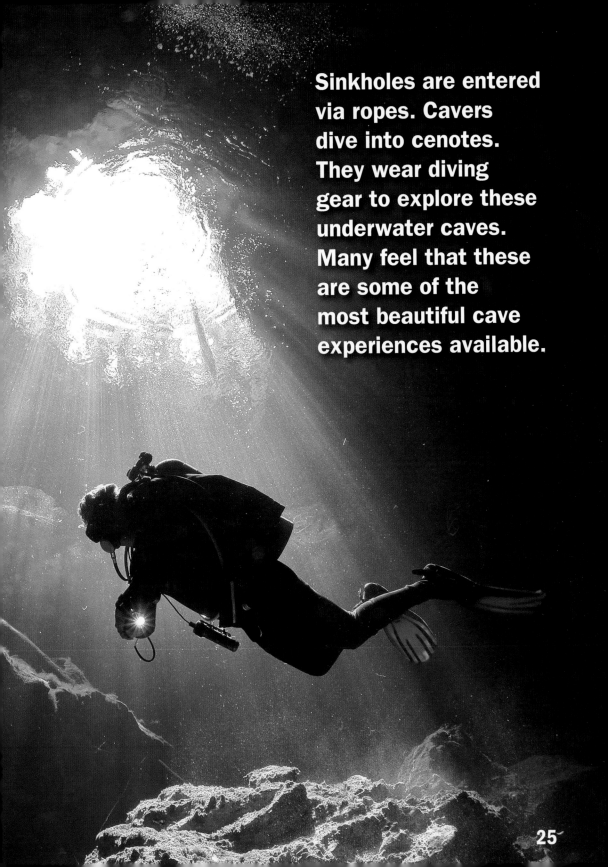

Sinkholes are entered via ropes. Cavers dive into cenotes. They wear diving gear to explore these underwater caves. Many feel that these are some of the most beautiful cave experiences available.

MUD & BOULDER CAVES

Mud caves are rare. They form when water digs out a narrow channel in the rock.

The channel fills in from landslides. Later, additional floodwaters wear away the lower debris and leave behind a muddy cave. California's Anza Borrego State Park is known for its mud caves.

Boulder caves are also known as talus caves. They are openings underneath and behind a stack of boulders. Boulders stack up after a rockslide. Water running in and around the boulders wears away the soft earth and creates a cave.

FORMATIONS & CAVE LIFE

Most caves have some type of stalactite or stalagmite formations. There are also some rare discoveries. Popcorn, bacon, pearls, and parachutes are just a few of the unusual and delicate formations found in caves. There are also mammals, amphibians, crustaceans, and arachnids that only live in caves. Cavers are careful to explore, map, and photograph while protecting a cave and its wildlife.

Popcorn Formation

Bacon Formation

Cave Pearls

Parachute Shield

Mexican Free-Tailed Bats,
Carlsbad Caverns, New Mexico

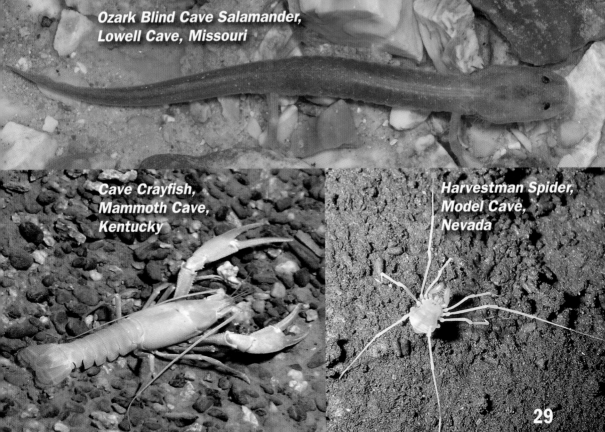

Ozark Blind Cave Salamander,
Lowell Cave, Missouri

Cave Crayfish,
Mammoth Cave,
Kentucky

Harvestman Spider,
Model Cave,
Nevada

29

GLOSSARY

ANASAZI
Ancient Native American people, some of whom once lived in sandstone caves in the southwestern United States.

ARACHNIDS
A class of living things that includes spiders and scorpions.

CAVE FORMATIONS
A unique form, such as a stalactite or stalagmite, created by minerals being deposited within a cave.

CRAMPON
A metal plate with sharp spikes that attaches to boots. Crampons are used by cavers and mountaineers to walk on ice without slipping.

GLACIER
An immense sheet of ice. Melting and dripping water may create a cave within the frozen ice sheet.

SPELUNKING
To explore a cave. Another word for caving. A spelunker is a person who explorers caves.

STALACTITES

An icicle-like formation that hangs from the ceiling of a cave. It is formed from the mineral calcite being left behind as water drips down from above.

STALAGMITES

A pointed formation that grows up from the ground of a cave. It is created as calcite-rich water drips down from a cave's roof, deposits on the floor, and builds upward.

TALUS CAVE

Another name for a boulder cave. Talus caves form when rocks drop down into a pile and openings are worn away under the rocks.

INDEX